D0052774

LESSONS ON ASSURANCE

A MINISTRY OF THE NAVIGATORS
P.O. Box 20, Colorado Springs, Colorado 80901

The Navigators is an international, evangelical Christian organization. Jesus Christ gave his followers the Great Commission to go and make disciples (Matthew 28:19). The aim of The Navigators is to help fulfill that commission by multiplying laborers for Christ in every nation.

NavPress is the publishing ministry of The Navigators. NavPress publications are tools to help Christians grow. Although publications alone cannot make disciples or change lives, they can help believers learn biblical discipleship, and apply what they learn to their lives and ministries.

© 1957, 1975, and 1980 by The Navigators
All rights reserved, including translation
ISBN: 0-89109-160-2

Scripture quotations are from the *New International Version,* © 1978 by the New York International Bible Society.

Printed in the United States of America

To assure is to "put beyond all doubt." *Lessons on Assurance* will help to assure you or "put you beyond all doubt" regarding some basic promises God has made to Christians. You can become convinced of the reality of these promises in your life as you memorize, meditate on, study, and apply the Scripture verses presented here.

Always memorize the verse presented at the beginning of each lesson. (Use the verse cards in the back of this booklet.) You may want to begin by memorizing the verse, or you may prefer to do the study questions about the verse first. In either case, be sure to memorize the topic and the reference as well as the verse. (The topic for each verse is the same as the lesson title in this book.)

One good way to memorize these is to quote the topic and reference at the beginning of the verse, and the reference at the end of the verse. For example, in quoting the verse in Lesson 1 you would say, "Assurance of Salvation, First John five, eleven and twelve," and then repeat the verse. At the end you would repeat the reference again.

Learn one phrase at a time. Say "Assurance of Salvation, First John five, eleven and twelve, 'And this is the testimony . . . .'" Repeat this several times until you know it. Then, repeating what you have just learned, add the next phrase: "Assurance of Salvation, First John five, eleven and twelve, 'And this is the testimony: God has given us eternal life. . . .'" Repeat all of this several times until you know it. Then add the next phrase. Repeat the process until you have memorized the verse.

In the back of this workbook are Scripture memory cards containing thirteen verses or passages from the *New International Version* of the Bible. If you prefer to memorize verses in another translation, you can write out the verses on the reverse side of the cards.

An essential part of Scripture memory is review. Review,

3

review, review! This will help you retain what you have memorized. Be sure to review each verse daily. You can take advantage of spare moments by carrying the verse cards you have learned wherever you go.

In each lesson you will:

- Memorize a verse.
- Think over what the verse says and means, and answer questions about it.
- Study other related passages.
- Write out the verse from memory.
- Write out a way to apply the verse to your everyday life.

Going through this process of memorizing, meditating, studying, and applying will help you understand and live by the principles presented in the verses.

1
ASSURANCE OF SALVATION

MEMORIZE 1 JOHN 5:11-12

Assurance of Salvation
     And this is the testimony: God has given us eternal life, and this life is in his Son. He who has the Son has life; he who does not have the Son of God does not have life.

1 John 5:11-12

The five verses you will memorize and study in *Lessons on Assurance* will equip you for your first encounters with the enemy. His first approach is often to cast doubt on the work God has done in your heart. Although you won't hear his audible voice, he will whisper this in your mind:

"You don't think you are saved and your sins forgiven just by believing and receiving Christ? Surely that is not enough!"

What will your answer be? Your only hope of successfully resisting such an attack is to resort to God's word. What does God say about the matter? That is the important thing for you to know.

On the basis of this "testimony"—God's written word— you can be convinced you have the Lord Jesus Christ, and with him eternal life. You can thus overcome in this first test of your faith. The attack may recur, but now you can meet it with the word of God in your heart.

EXPLORING 1 JOHN 5:11-12

Who gives eternal life?

Where is eternal life found?

5

Who has eternal life?

_____

Who does not have eternal life?

_____

"THIS IS THE TESTIMONY"

1. What did John say in John 20:31 about why he wrote this book?

_____

_____

"GOD HAS GIVEN US ETERNAL LIFE"

2. According to Romans 5:8, how has God shown that he loves you?

_____

_____

3. What results of man's sinfulness are listed in Isaiah 59:2?

_____

_____

SINFUL MAN

HOLY GOD

DEATH

SIN SEPARATES

ETERNAL LIFE

4. Read Ephesians 2:8-9. Why do human efforts always fail to reach God?

_____

_____

_____

_____

_____

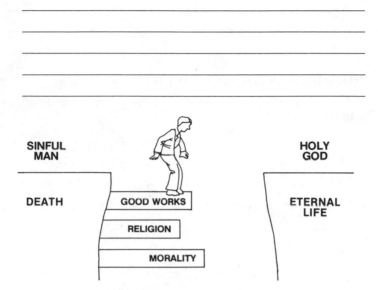

5. In 1 Peter 3:18 how did Peter explain what God has done to bring men to himself?

_____

_____

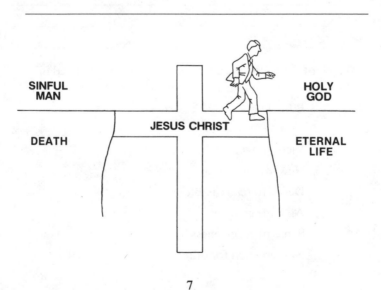

6. How did John say a person receives the gift of salvation in John 1:12?

_____

_____

_____

"HE WHO HAS THE SON HAS LIFE"

7. According to John 5:24, what three things are the result of hearing and believing?

PRESENT _____

FUTURE _____

PAST _____

8. What did Jesus promise his followers in John 10:27-29?

_____

_____

_____

9. What takes place when a person becomes a Christian, as described in 2 Corinthians 5:17?

_____

_____

_____

Which of the following changes have you experienced in your life? (Check appropriate ones.)

___ Inner peace

___ New awareness of sin

___ Victory over sin

___ New love for God

___ Desire to read the Bible

___ Attitude changes

___ Sense of forgiveness

___ New concern for others

8

WRITE OUT 1 JOHN 5:11-12 FROM MEMORY.

_____

_____

_____

_____

_____

_____

APPLYING 1 JOHN 5:11-12

Meditate on 1 John 5:11-12 and consider how to apply it to your life.

How do you know that you have eternal life?

_____

_____

_____

Now take a few moments to thank God for all he has given you in Jesus Christ.

2
ASSURANCE OF ANSWERED PRAYER

Review 1 John 5:11-12, and check here ____ after quoting it correctly from memory.

MEMORIZE JOHN 16:24

Assurance of Answered Prayer
"Until now you have not asked for anything in my name. Ask and you will receive, and your joy will be complete."

John 16:24

Another attack of Satan may be to cause you to doubt the effectiveness of prayer. He may whisper to you, "You don't think God is really personally interested in you? He's far away, and concerned about more important things. Surely you don't think he'll hear your prayers—much less answer them!"

But with Jesus Christ as your Savior and Lord, you have the unique privilege of speaking directly with your heavenly Father through him. God wants you to come confidently into his presence through Christ and to talk to him about everything (look up Philippians 4:6 and Hebrews 4:14-16). He is intensely interested in you and your needs.

In the memory verse for this lesson, John 16:24, Jesus was speaking to his disciples the night before his crucifixion. He did not tell them they had never before asked for anything in prayer. But he said they had not asked *in his name.* You yourself have probably prayed many times, especially when in trouble. But as a believer in Christ you can ask in Jesus' name, because you belong to him. To ask in his name means to ask in his authority and on his merit. Just as the Father answered Jesus' every prayer, so he will answer you when you ask in Jesus' name.

11

Memorize this promise, apply its truth, and experience the joy of answered prayer.

EXPLORING JOHN 16:24

What is prayer?

talking with God.

In whose name should you pray?

Jesus

What results from prayer?

"UNTIL NOW YOU HAVE NOT ASKED FOR ANYTHING IN MY NAME"

1. What does Jesus teach about prayer in Matthew 7:7-8?

Prayer is answered

2. What are some important conditions for answered prayer?

John 15:7

Live in God — God in me.

1 John 5:14-15

Ask according to God's will.

"ASK AND YOU WILL RECEIVE"

3. What is characteristic of God's answers to prayer?

Jeremiah 33:3

Knowledge of great things

Ephesians 3:20

More than is asked.

12

4. Read Matthew 7:9-11. What kind of gifts does God give his children?

Good gifts - the best

How do you think God would respond to a request for something he knew would be bad for you?

He wouldn't give it.

What do you think God would do if he knew the answer would be better for you at another time?

Delay it.

5. Read Philippians 4:6-7. What is the wrong reaction to have toward difficult circumstances?

to get worried

What is the right response?

take it to God in prayer

What is the result of this right response?

Internal peace greater than any peace (incomprehensible)

"YOUR JOY WILL BE COMPLETE"

6. From Philippians 4:7, what results from the peace that comes through prayer?

Keeps us safe.

7. Read Luke 1:13-14. What resulted when Zechariah and Elizabeth prayed for a son?

they received a son

8. What are some hindrances to answered prayer? James 4:3

wrong motives - selfish pleasures

Psalm 66:18

unclean heart.

13

WRITE OUT JOHN 16:24 FROM MEMORY.

Joh 16:24 Until now you have asked for nothing in my name. Ask and it shall be given you and your joy will be made complete

Four important areas of prayer are:

ADORATION —reflecting on God himself. Praise him for his love, his power and majesty, and his wonderful gift of Christ.

CONFESSION —admitting your sins to God. Be honest and humble. Remember he knows you and loves you still.

THANKSGIVING —telling God how grateful you are for everything he has given—even the unpleasant things. Your thankfulness will help you see his purposes.

SUPPLICATION —making specific requests, both for others and for yourself.

The first letters of these four words form the word "ACTS." Use this as a mental guide for a balanced prayer life.

APPLYING JOHN 16:24

List four specific things you can pray about today. Pause right now and talk to God about them.

ADORATION

_____

_____

CONFESSION

_____

_____

THANKSGIVING

_____

_____

SUPPLICATION

_____

_____

14

3
ASSURANCE
OF VICTORY

Review the following verses, and check them off after quoting them correctly from memory.

1 John 5:11-12____   John 16:24____

MEMORIZE 1 CORINTHIANS 10:13

Assurance of Victory
No temptation has seized you except what is common to man. And God is faithful; he will not let you be tempted beyond what you can bear. But when you are tempted, he will also provide a way out so that you can stand up under it.

1 Corinthians 10:13

Still another attack from Satan may be along this line: He will whisper to you, "You have life, all right, but you are a weakling; you have always been a weakling."

He will remind you of some sin which has gripped you for years. He will point to something of which you are keenly aware, and say, "You are weak, and you will not be able to stand against this temptation. You may be able to stand against others, but not this one."

How will you answer him? Will you attempt to reason? Will you try to produce your own arguments? Will you run to see what other people say? Or will you resort to the invincible word of God?

Knowing 1 Corinthians 10:13 will allow you to ward off this attack. God promises victory. It belongs to you as his child. Believe him, and you will see how God does things that are impossible with men. It will thrill you to see chains of lifetime habits broken by his mighty power.

EXPLORING 1 CORINTHIANS 10:13

What is true about every temptation you face?

_____

_____

Who can give you victory when you are tempted?

_____

_____

Does God remove temptation?

_____

What does God do for you?

_____

_____

"TEMPTATION . . . IS COMMON TO MAN"

1. What is a major source of temptation that James described in James 1:13-14?

_____

_____

_____

2. Read 1 John 2:15-16. What are three primary areas of temptation?

_____

_____

_____

3. According to Peter's statement in 1 Peter 5:8, what is the devil seeking to do when he tempts you?

_____

What does this mean to you?

_____

_____

_____

_____

Your choice: to escape temptation,
or to fall into sin.

"GOD IS FAITHFUL"

4. What does God do for you, according to 2 Thessalonians
   3:3?

   _____

5. What does Hebrews 4:15 tell you about Jesus Christ?

   _____

   _____

"A WAY OUT"

6. What are some things you can do to keep temptation from
   leading into sin?

   Matthew 6:9,13

   _____

Psalm 119:9,11

_____

1 John 5:4-5

_____

Hebrews 4:16

_____

James 4:7

_____

WRITE OUT 1 CORINTHIANS 10:13 FROM MEMORY.

_____

_____

_____

_____

_____

_____

_____

APPLYING 1 CORINTHIANS 10:13

What is a temptation that frequently seizes you?

_____

What do you think God's way of escape is?

_____

_____

_____

4

ASSURANCE OF FORGIVENESS

Review the following verses, and check them off after quoting them correctly from memory.

1 John 5:11-12___   1 Corinthians 10:13___
John 16:24___

MEMORIZE 1 JOHN 1:9

Assurance of Forgiveness
    If we confess our sins, he is faithful and just and will forgive us our sins and purify us from all unrighteousness.

1 John 1:9

Although victory over sin is rightfully yours, there will be times when you miss the way of escape. You will fail and sin against God. Once you do, your enemy will be on the job immediately:
    "Now you've done it. Aren't you supposed to be a Christian? Christians don't do those things."
    But God makes provision in his word for the failures of his children, as we see in 1 John 1:9. We receive his full forgiveness as we confess to him our sins.
    To confess a sin means to uncover it and call it exactly what God calls it. This honest confession must include the willingness to forsake the sin. God promises not only to forgive us, but also to cleanse us from all unrighteousness. What a gracious provision!

EXPLORING 1 JOHN 1:9

What does God want you to do about your sins?

_____

_____

What does it mean to confess?

_____

_____

_____

In his act of forgiving us, how is God described?

_____

What else does God do when you confess your sins?

_____

"IF WE CONFESS OUR SINS"

1. Read 1 John 1:8,10. What did John say you should recognize about yourself?

_____

_____

2. What should be your attitude toward sin?

Psalm 139:23-24

_____

Psalm 38:18

_____

3. What should accompany your confession of sin, according to Proverbs 28:13?

_____

_____

"HE IS FAITHFUL AND JUST
AND WILL FORGIVE . . . AND PURIFY"

4. How is God described in Psalm 86:5?

_____

_____

5. According to Ephesians 1:7, on what basis are you forgiven?

_____

6. What does Hebrews 10:12 say about Christ's sacrifice?

_____

7. Read Hebrews 10:17. Why is it foolish for you to continue to feel guilty about sin?

_____

_____

8. According to Ephesians 4:32 what should be your attitude toward those who have offended you? Why?

_____

_____

_____

WRITE OUT 1 JOHN 1:9 FROM MEMORY.

_____

_____

_____

_____

APPLYING 1 JOHN 1:9

Perhaps as you worked on this lesson something came to your mind which is hindering your fellowship with God—some sin you have committed for which you have not asked forgiveness. If so, write down what God brought to your mind.

_____

Confess this to God, and claim the promise of 1 John 1:9 that he has forgiven your sin. Thank him for his forgiveness.

21

5

ASSURANCE
OF GUIDANCE

Review the following verses, and check them off after quoting them correctly from memory.

1 John 5:11-12___   1 Corinthians 10:13___
John 16:24___   1 John 1:9___

MEMORIZE PROVERBS 3:5-6

Assurance of Guidance
    Trust in the Lord with all your heart and lean not on your own understanding; in all your ways acknowledge him, and he will make your paths straight.

Proverbs 3:5-6

You may have questions about the future, wondering how this new life of yours is going to work out. What about God's will for your life? Will he really lead you?
    God does promise to lead you as you rely on him completely. He can guide you perfectly, for he knows all your needs, and has infinite wisdom, power, and riches to give you the best life possible.
    He deserves your trust.

EXPLORING PROVERBS 3:5-6

What three things are you told to do?

_____

_____

_____

When these conditions are met, what are you promised?

_____

"TRUST IN THE LORD"

1. Read Psalm 32:8. What can you trust God to do for you?

_____

_____

2. According to Romans 12:1-2, what steps should be taken to experience God's will?

_____

_____

_____

_____

How is God's will described?

_____

_____

3. To whom does God promise special blessing in Jeremiah 17:7?

_____

_____

"LEAN NOT ON YOUR OWN UNDERSTANDING"

4. What warning does God give in Jeremiah 17:5?

_____

_____

5. Read Isaiah 55:8-9. Why should we not limit ourselves to human understanding?

_____

_____

_____

6. What principle, described in John 6:38, did Jesus follow in making decisions?

_____

_____

"IN ALL YOUR WAYS ACKNOWLEDGE HIM"

7. List some of the "ways" of your life in which you need to acknowledge God (for example: spending money, your job, leisure time).

_____

_____

_____

_____

_____

_____

Select one of them, and tell how you can better acknowledge
God in this area.

_____

_____

"HE WILL MAKE YOUR PATHS STRAIGHT"

8. What means has God provided for determining his will?
   Psalm 119:105

   _____

   1 Corinthians 2:12

   _____

9. Read James 1:5. What should you do about situations you
   don't understand?

   _____

   How are you to ask? (James 1:6-7)

   _____

10. What precedes the fulfillment of God's promises, according
    to Hebrews 10:36?

    _____

WRITE OUT PROVERBS 3:5-6 FROM MEMORY.

_____

_____

_____

_____

_____

_____

25

APPLYING PROVERBS 3:5-6

Describe a situation in your life in which you are seeking God's guidance.

_____

_____

_____

List ways that show how you can trust God in this situation.

_____

_____

_____

_____

_____

SCRIPTURE PASSAGES
USED IN *LESSONS ON ASSURANCE*

Psalm 32:8   I will instruct you and teach you in the way you should go; I will counsel you and watch over you.

Psalm 38:18   I confess my iniquity; I am troubled by my sin.

Psalm 66:18   If I had cherished sin in my heart, the Lord would not have listened.

Psalm 86:5   You are kind and forgiving, O Lord, abounding in love to all who call to you.

Psalm 119:9-11   ⁹How can a young man keep his way pure? By living according to your word. ¹⁰I seek you with all my heart; do not let me stray from your commands. ¹¹I have hidden your word in my heart that I might not sin against you.

Psalm 199:105   Your word is a lamp to my feet and a light for my path.

Psalm 139:23-24   ²³Search me, O God, and know my heart; test me and know my anxious thoughts. ²⁴See if there is any offensive way in me, and lead me in the way everlasting.

Proverbs 28:13   He who conceals his sins does not prosper, but whoever confesses and renounces them finds mercy.

Isaiah 55:8-9   ⁸"For my thoughts are not your thoughts, neither are your ways my ways," declares the Lord. ⁹"As the heavens are higher than the earth, so are my ways higher than your ways and my thoughts than your thoughts."

Isaiah 59:2	But your iniquities have separated you from your God; your sins have hidden his face from you, so that he will not hear.
Jeremiah 17:5	This is what the Lord says: "Cursed is the one who trusts in man, who depends on flesh for his strength and whose heart turns away from the Lord."
Jeremiah 17:7	"But blessed is the man who trusts in the Lord, whose confidence is in him."
Matthew 6:9-13	9"This is how you should pray: 'Our Father in heaven, hallowed be your name, 10your kingdom come, your will be done on earth as it is in heaven. 11Give us today our daily bread. 12Forgive us our debts, as we also have forgiven our debtors. 13And lead us not into temptation, but deliver us from the evil one.'"
Matthew 7:7-11	7"Ask and it will be given to you; seek and you will find; knock and the door will be opened to you. 8For everyone who asks receives; he who seeks finds; and to him who knocks, the door will be opened. 9Which of you, if his son asks for bread, will give him a stone? 10Or if he asks for a fish, will give him a snake? 11If you, then, though you are evil, know how to give good gifts to your children, how much more will your Father in heaven give good gifts to those who ask him!"
Luke 1:13-14	13But the angel said to him: "Do not be afraid, Zechariah; your prayer has been heard. Your wife Elizabeth will bear you a son, and you are to give him the name John. 14He will be a joy and delight to you, and many will rejoice because of his birth."
John 1:12	Yet to all who received him, to those who believed in his name, he gave the right to become children of God.
John 5:24	"I tell you the truth, whoever hears my word and believes him who sent me has

eternal life and will not be condemned; he has crossed over from death to life.''

John 6:38
''For I have come down from heaven not to do my will but to do the will of him who sent me.''

John 10:27-29
[27]''My sheep listen to my voice; I know them, and they follow me. [28]I give them eternal life, and they shall never perish; no one can snatch them out of my hand. [29]My Father, who has given them to me, is greater than all; no one can snatch them out of my Father's hand.''

John 15:7
''If you remain in me and my words remain in you, ask whatever you wish, and it will be given you.''

John 20:30-31
[30]Jesus did many other miraculous signs in the presence of his disciples, which are not recorded in this book. [31]But these are written that you may believe that Jesus is the Christ, the Son of God, and that by believing you may have life in his name.

Romans 5:8
God demonstrates his own love for us in this: While we were still sinners, Christ died for us.

Romans 12:1-2
[1]Therefore, I urge you, brothers, in view of God's mercy, to offer your bodies as living sacrifices, holy and pleasing to God— which is your spiritual worship. [2]Do not conform any longer to the pattern of this world, but be transformed by the renewing of your mind. Then you will be able to test and approve what God's will is—his good, pleasing and perfect will.

1 Corinthians 2:12
We have not received the spirit of the world but the Spirit who is from God, that we may understand what God has freely given us.

2 Corinthians 5:17
Therefore, if anyone is in Christ, he is a new creation; the old has gone, the new has come!

29

Ephesians 1:7	In him we have redemption through his blood, the forgiveness of sins, in accordance with the riches of God's grace.
Ephesians 2:8-9	[8]For it is by grace you have been saved, through faith—and this not from yourselves, it is the the gift of God—[9]not by works, so that no one can boast.
Ephesians 3:20-21	[20]Now to him who is able to do immeasurably more than all we ask or imagine, according to his power that is at work within us, [21]to him be glory in the church and in Christ Jesus throughout all generations, for ever and ever!
Ephesians 4:32	Be kind and compassionate to one another, forgiving each other, just as in Christ God forgave you.
Philippians 4:6-7	[6]Do not be anxious about anything, but in everything, by prayer and petition, with thanksgiving, present your requests to God. [7]And the peace of God, which transcends all understanding, will guard your hearts and your minds in Christ Jesus.
2 Thessalonians 3:3	The Lord is faithful, and he will strengthen and protect you from the evil one.
Hebrews 4:14-16	[14]Therefore, since we have a great high priest who has gone through the heavens, Jesus the Son of God, let us hold firmly to the faith we profess. [15]For we do not have a high priest who is unable to sympathize with our weaknesses, but we have one who has been tempted in every way, just as we are—yet was without sin. [16]Let us then approach the throne of grace with confidence, so that we may receive mercy and find grace to help us in our time of need.
Hebrews 10:12	But when this priest had offered for all time one sacrifice for sins, he sat down at the right hand of God.
Hebrews 10:17	"Their sins and lawless acts I will remember no more."

Hebrews 10:36 You need to persevere so that when you have done the will of God, you will receive what he has promised.

James 1:5-8 ⁵If any of you lacks wisdom, he should ask God, who gives generously to all without finding fault, and it will be given to him. ⁶But when he asks, he must believe and not doubt, because he who doubts is like a wave of the sea, blown and tossed by the wind. ⁷That man should not think he will receive anything from the Lord; ⁸he is a double-minded man, unstable in all he does.

James 1:13-14 ¹³When tempted, no one should say, "God is tempting me." For God cannot be tempted by evil, nor does he tempt anyone; ¹⁴but each one is tempted when, by his own evil desire, he is dragged away and enticed.

James 4:3 When you ask, you do not receive, because you ask with wrong motives, that you may spend what you get on your pleasures.

James 4:7 Submit yourselves, then, to God. Resist the devil, and he will flee from you.

1 Peter 3:18 For Christ died for sins once for all, the righteous for the unrighteous, to bring you to God. He was put to death in the body but made alive by the Spirit.

1 Peter 5:8 Be self-controlled and alert. Your enemy the devil prowls around like a roaring lion looking for someone to devour.

1 John 1:8-10 ⁸If we claim to be without sin, we deceive ourselves and the truth is not in us. ⁹If we confess our sins, he is faithful and just and will forgive us our sins and purify us from all unrighteousness. ¹⁰If we claim we have not sinned, we make him out to be a liar and his word has no place in our lives.

1 John 2:15-16 ¹⁵Do not love the world or anything in the world. If anyone loves the world, the love of the Father is not in him. ¹⁶For everything in the world—the cravings of sinful man, the lust of his eyes and the boasting of what he has and does—comes not from the Father but from the world.

1 John 5:4-5

[4]Everyone born of God has overcome the world. This is the victory that has overcome the world, even our faith. [5]Who is it that overcomes the world? Only he who believes that Jesus is the Son of God.

1 John 5:14-15

[14]This is the assurance we have in approaching God: that if we ask anything according to his will, he hears us. [15]And if we know that he hears us—whatever we ask—we know that we have what we asked of him.